READ-TOGETHER TREASURY

CLASSIC STORIES

publications international, ltd.

A NOTE ABOUT THIS READ-TOGETHER TREASURY

This is a special book. It is designed and written to be shared between an experienced reader and a beginning reader, taking turns reading aloud.

The treasury is extra-wide so that it can be easily spread across two laps. The experienced reader—Mom or Dad, Grandma or Grandpa, even an older brother or sister—sits on the left and reads aloud the left-hand pages. These pages are written using the classic storybook prose that children love to hear, but may not yet be able to read on their own.

The beginning reader sits on the right and reads aloud the right-hand pages. These pages are written especially for early readers. The type is larger and less intimidating, the vocabulary is basic, and the sentences are short and simple.

This book provides the perfect opportunity for a young reader to hone his or her reading and comprehension skills. The positive experience of reading together with a loved one will encourage a love of reading in children. And the quality time spent as you take turns reading may be the greatest reward of all.

Please enjoy this unique book, full of stories to read aloud, stories to treasure...stories to share.

Between the dark and the daylight,

When the night is beginning to lower,

Comes a pause in the day's occupations,

That is known as the Children's Hour.

—Henry Wadsworth Longfellow

"The Children's Hour"

TABLE OF CONTENTS

Gulliver's Travels

Based on the original story by Jonathan Swift

Adapted by Lynne Roberts   Illustrated by Karen Stormer Brooks

In London there lived a man named Gulliver. He was a doctor and had a wife and family. Overall, he had a very ordinary life. But Gulliver did not want an ordinary life. He longed for adventure. He wanted to sail the high seas.

One day, Gulliver saw a sign for a ship that needed a doctor. He knew this was his chance to travel far away from England. He quickly signed up to be the ship's doctor.

The ship sailed the ocean for several months when it was hit by a violent storm. Giant waves crashed into the boat, sending it far off course. Soon the ship hit some jagged rocks and was torn apart. Gulliver was thrown into the cold ocean water.

Gulliver woke up suddenly. He remembered being on the ship. He remembered that the ship sank. But he did not remember swimming to land.

Gulliver tried to get up. He could not move. He was tied down by many thin ropes. Gulliver felt a tickle as a few tiny men crawled on his chest.

As Gulliver raised his hand in fright, a few of the ropes broke. The tiny men around Gulliver then began to shoot little arrows, like pins, at Gulliver.

Gulliver realized that the tiny people were frightened of him. The tiny people felt threatened that he would crush them. Gulliver was not a violent man. He wanted to be friends with these little people. He listened quietly as they spoke to him in a strange language.

Soon the little people were bringing lumber from all around. They began to build an enormous platform with wheels. When the cart was completed, it took nine hundred little people to lift Gulliver onto the cart. It then took them all day and half of the next to pull Gulliver to the main city, which was only half a mile away.

At the main city, Gulliver met a man whom he presumed to be the emperor. Gulliver wasn't sure what the emperor was saying, but he came to understand that he was in a place called Lilliput. The people were called Lilliputians. After many weeks of listening to the Lilliputians, Gulliver began to understand the language of Lilliput.

Gulliver liked the emperor. He showed him his pocket watch. The watch was as big as the emperor. The tick-tick of the watch hurt the emperor's ears. Gulliver kindly put the watch away. He kept it safely in his pocket.

The emperor trusted Gulliver. He told Gulliver about a place called Blefuscu.

The emperor of Blefuscu and the emperor of Lilliput had a fight. They did not agree about which end of an egg should be cracked first. The emperor of Lilliput wanted Gulliver to help fight Blefuscu.

Since Gulliver was not a violent man, he did not want to do battle with Blefuscu. He listened as the emperor explained where the island of Blefuscu was. Gulliver realized that he could easily swim to the island. He soon had a great plan.

Gulliver took the strongest ropes that he could find in Lilliput. He fashioned them to the toughest steel anchors and set out toward Blefuscu. All the Blefuscan ships were lined up by the Blefuscan shore. Gulliver swam underwater until he was close to the ships. Then he popped out of the water.

The Blefuscan army was stunned by this giant man who emerged from the sea. Gulliver quickly attached the ropes and anchors to the Blefuscan ships. He then pulled the whole fleet of ships toward the Lilliputian shore. When Gulliver arrived back at Lilliput with the Blefuscan ships in tow, the Lilliputians and the emperor cheered. Gulliver was a hero!

But even a hero gets sad. Gulliver wanted to go home. One day, Gulliver found a boat that was his size. Gulliver jumped into the boat and rowed away.

A few days later, Gulliver was picked up by an English ship. Gulliver was so happy to see people his own size!

Gulliver told the crew about Lilliput. They did not believe his story. Then Gulliver took two tiny cows out of his pocket. The crew of the English ship soon believed every word of Gulliver's story.

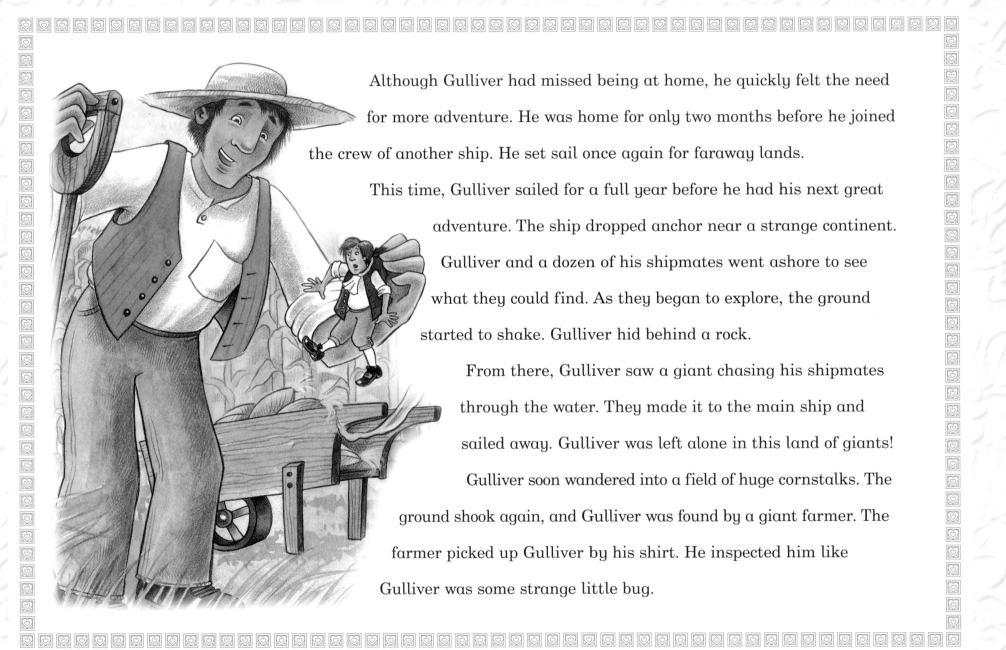

Although Gulliver had missed being at home, he quickly felt the need for more adventure. He was home for only two months before he joined the crew of another ship. He set sail once again for faraway lands.

This time, Gulliver sailed for a full year before he had his next great adventure. The ship dropped anchor near a strange continent. Gulliver and a dozen of his shipmates went ashore to see what they could find. As they began to explore, the ground started to shake. Gulliver hid behind a rock.

From there, Gulliver saw a giant chasing his shipmates through the water. They made it to the main ship and sailed away. Gulliver was left alone in this land of giants!

Gulliver soon wandered into a field of huge cornstalks. The ground shook again, and Gulliver was found by a giant farmer. The farmer picked up Gulliver by his shirt. He inspected him like Gulliver was some strange little bug.

The farmer took Gulliver home. Gulliver met the farmer's family. Even the baby was a giant!

The farmer's daughter liked to dress up Gulliver like a doll. She taught Gulliver that he was in a land called Brobdingnag.

The farmer had an idea. He knew he could make money by showing off this little man he found. He took Gulliver to the market.

The farmer made Gulliver sing and dance for money. People came from all over to see the tiny man.

One of the people who came to see Gulliver perform was the queen of Brobdingnag. She was very impressed with this little man. She offered the farmer a lot of money to buy Gulliver for her private collection. Gulliver agreed to go with the queen only if the farmer's daughter could come along, too, to be Gulliver's teacher and friend. The queen accepted and gave the farmer's daughter a job at the palace.

The queen was so delighted with her new little man. She showed him to all her friends. They all giggled as they watched Gulliver eat a tiny meal off of a tiny plate on a tiny table, all fashioned especially for Gulliver's use. The queen also had a small box made for Gulliver. This box had several tiny rooms and was furnished with only the finest trimmings found around the palace.

Gulliver sat on a spool of gold thread and slept on a fine silk handkerchief. Gulliver's box also had handles so that he could be carried. The farmer's daughter took him to the beach to watch the waves, or to the garden to walk among the flowers.

The king did not like Gulliver as much as the queen did. He thought the little man was boring. Not even the sound of Gulliver's piano playing could make the king happy.

One day, Gulliver was in his box on the beach. He sat quietly and watched the waves from one of the windows.

Suddenly, he was up in the air. An eagle had picked up the box!

The eagle flew over the ocean and dropped the box into the water. Gulliver was now on his way to his next adventure!

The Call of the Wild

Based on the original story by Jack London

Adapted by Elizabeth Olson   Illustrated by Jane Maday

Buck lived in the sunny southland at Judge Miller's place. From the top of the hill he watched over the judge's property. He could see the red barn and the distant fields.

Buck had a good life. He spent long days enjoying the southland's fine weather. He rolled in the grass or stretched his legs by running through the fields. His strong legs, capable of great speed, never tired. On cool evenings Buck lay at the judge's feet near the warm fire in the house.

Other animals on the farm had jobs to do. The horses pulled plows and the cows gave milk. But Buck did as he pleased. His regal bearing announced to everyone that he was his own master.

One day when the judge was gone, a man stole Buck. The man put Buck in a cage. "Sit, Buck," he said. "You are going on a long trip."

The man put the cage on a train car. He shut the door. Buck felt the train move forward. Then Buck felt the train move faster. The train chugged along the rails for many days. Buck felt the air grow colder.

One day the train chugged to a stop. The conductor opened the door. Cold air blew on Buck's face.

Everywhere he looked, Buck saw dogs and white ground. He jumped from the train car. His feet sank into the white mush. Surprised, he sprang backward.

More of the white stuff fell from the sky. Buck opened his mouth. A cold sting hit his tongue and disappeared. "Where did it go?" Buck wondered.

A man wearing a hat with a tassel knelt down beside Buck. "This must be your first snow," the man said, patting Buck kindly. "You're in the northland now, and you belong to me. You will help me deliver the mail." The man put a piece of meat in front of Buck. "Eat up," said the man. "You'll need your strength."

Buck ate hungrily. Afterward the man led Buck to a sled. He hooked an arrangement of straps and buckles onto Buck. It was a harness, just as Buck had seen the horses wear at Judge Miller's place. The man fastened four dogs in front of Buck and one behind him. Buck did not know what to do.

"Don't worry," said Dave, a big yellow dog behind him. "I'll help you."

"Mush!" called the man. All six dogs pulled. They pulled as hard as they could. The sled slowly moved forward.

"Mush!" called the man again. Buck pulled with all his might. The sled picked up speed. The sled moved faster and faster. Soon the dogs ran along the trail. The sled raced along behind them.

Dave told Buck how to keep the sled in its tracks. Dave also told Buck how to keep clear of the sled when it shot downhill behind them. A quick learner, Buck soon pulled the sled as well as the other dogs.

For many weeks, the sled team traveled across the northland. The man with the tasseled hat and the six dogs worked hard to deliver the mail.

From Dave and the other dogs, Buck learned how to live in the cold northland. But his paws were not as hard as those of the other dogs. Buck began to limp in pain from his long days on the trail. One evening he did not even rise to receive his ration of meat.

"You poor fella," said the man. "I'll bring your food to you." The man set the meat near Buck's mouth. "Tomorrow I'll have a surprise for you. You won't have this problem anymore."

The next day when the man strapped Buck into the harness, he placed four tiny moccasins on Buck's paws. "I made these from my own shoes," he said. "They will protect your paws until they become stronger." Buck wore the moccasins for several weeks. Eventually the shoes fell away, but by that time Buck no longer needed them. His paws were tough enough for the trail.

One day the dogs crossed a patch of thin ice. The lead dog, Spitz, broke through the ice. He fell into the water. The harness pulled the next three dogs into the water, too.

"Buck! Dave!" called the man. "Pull backward!" Buck and Dave pulled with all their might. They quickly pulled all four dogs from the water.

"Good work, Dave and Buck!" said the man. "You saved the other dogs."

Buck liked the other dogs, especially Dave. Almost all of them liked him too. Buck's strength and speed made him a valuable member of the sled team. His regal bearing, well known at Judge Miller's place, made him stand out. Spitz, the lead dog in the harness, sensed Buck's superiority and felt threatened. The older, more experienced Spitz decided to put Buck in his place. One evening while Buck ate his ration of meat, he looked up at the moon. The glowing disk held his eyes for a few moments. Buck recalled his evenings by the fire in the southland. He remembered running in the fields. When he looked down, the meat was gone. A few yards away, he saw Spitz greedily eating his ration. "Dreamers don't deserve to eat," said Spitz.

The hair stood up on the back of Buck's neck. "I'll let you keep the meat," Buck said. "But if you bully me again, I'll defend myself. The northland is no place for weakness. And I won't show weakness toward you or anyone."

"You're no match for me," said Spitz angrily. "I'm the lead dog. I do as I want around here."

A few nights later, Buck dug a warm bed in the snow. Then he went for a short walk. When he came back, Spitz was in his bed. "I warned you," said Buck. "I will not let you bully me."

"I can do as I want," said Spitz. "I am the strongest dog on the team."

Buck sprang at Spitz. The two dogs rolled in the snow. Buck was stronger and faster. Spitz lost the fight. Buck was now the lead dog.

Buck led the team across the northland. His instincts became as sharp as those of a wild animal. If Buck caught the scent of a bear on the wind, he knew to direct the sled away from it. If the team began to lose control of the sled on a downhill slope, Buck knew to run toward an incline. The man in the tasseled hat trusted Buck's instincts and followed him.

As in his earlier life, Buck again carried himself as if he were his own master. He went where he pleased and did what he pleased. But he also liked to be with the man and to work for him. He helped the man deliver the mail in record time through some of the northland's snowiest days.

In the evenings, Buck sat by the fire at the man's feet. Buck looked into the flames and remembered the judge and his former home. He recalled the long days sitting at the top of the hill. He remembered rolling in the grass and running through the fields. He also thought of all that he had learned since coming northward.

Sometimes on the trail, Buck imagined that he followed an old path. He thought he could see the paw prints of dogs.

One night Buck joined the other dogs. They moved in the darkness beyond the fire. They howled at the moon.

They called to the dogs of long ago. They called to the dogs who had pulled sleds like the one they pulled now.

Buck knew that his new life was the right life for him. He was happy.

Buck lifted his head to the moon and howled.

Pocahontas

Based on the original story by Captain John Smith

Adapted by Lisa Harkrader   Illustrated by Karen Pritchett

"Pocahontas! Pocahontas, stay here beside our lodge."

"Yes, Mother." I waited until my mother returned to her cooking, then I crept to the edge of the village to watch the woods. That morning a young warrior from a neighboring tribe had come into the village. He spoke to my father, and now everyone in the village was bustling about. Something important was happening, and I didn't want to miss it.

I soon saw a line of warriors marching toward me through the thick woods. They were leading a prisoner—one of the Englishmen from the strange wooden village by the sea.

The prisoner was funny-looking. All the Englishmen were funny-looking. He had a bushy beard. His skin was light. His clothes were bulky. He did not paint himself with bear grease to keep warm.

Three warriors held his arms. Twenty other warriors guarded him. But he did not look scared.

The warriors led the strange man through the village. Then they led him to my father's lodge. My father was the most important man in our tribe. My father was chief of the Powhatan. He ruled over thirty tribes.

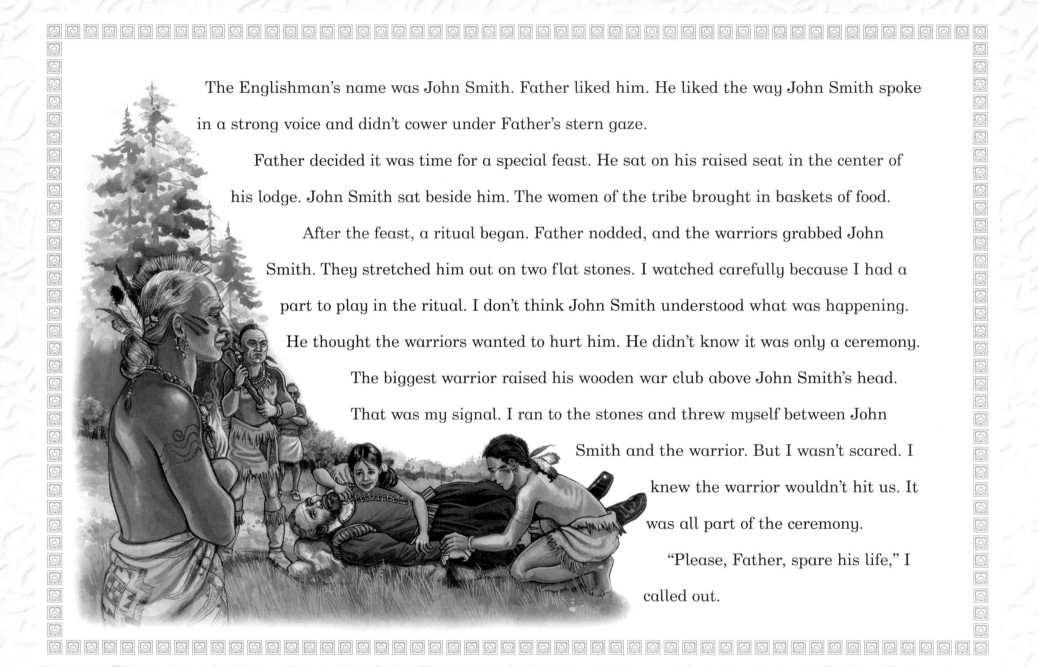

The Englishman's name was John Smith. Father liked him. He liked the way John Smith spoke in a strong voice and didn't cower under Father's stern gaze.

Father decided it was time for a special feast. He sat on his raised seat in the center of his lodge. John Smith sat beside him. The women of the tribe brought in baskets of food.

After the feast, a ritual began. Father nodded, and the warriors grabbed John Smith. They stretched him out on two flat stones. I watched carefully because I had a part to play in the ritual. I don't think John Smith understood what was happening. He thought the warriors wanted to hurt him. He didn't know it was only a ceremony.

The biggest warrior raised his wooden war club above John Smith's head. That was my signal. I ran to the stones and threw myself between John Smith and the warrior. But I wasn't scared. I knew the warrior wouldn't hit us. It was all part of the ceremony.

"Please, Father, spare his life," I called out.

Father nodded. The warriors let John Smith get up. John Smith was now part of our tribe. Soon John Smith went back to his own village.

Father decided to send some of our people to John Smith's village to trade food and furs. I wanted to go, too. "Please, Father," I said. "I could help. John Smith knows I am his friend."

"You may go, little playful one," said Father. That is what Pocahontas means: little playful one. When we arrived at John Smith's village, the Englishmen were glad to see us.

John Smith's village was called Jamestown. I visited there often. But my people and John Smith's people soon began fighting, and Father stopped sending food to Jamestown. I couldn't let the English starve. I sneaked food out of our village and gave it to them. I also warned them when the Powhatans were planning to attack.

The fighting between my people and the English grew worse, and I went to another Powhatan village to live. The chief of this village was named Jazapaws. He was friendly with the English.

One day Jazapaws told me that an Englishman, Captain Argall, had invited Jazapaws and his wife to have dinner aboard his ship. "He wants you to come, too," Jazapaws said.

Jazapaws and his wife took me to the ship. Captain Argall took my hand. "Welcome aboard the *Treasurer*," said Captain Argall.

"Thank you for inviting me," I said.

"I'm sorry," said Captain Argall, "but you must stay here until your father returns the Englishmen he captured."

"Do not worry, Pocahontas," said Captain Argall. "We will not harm you. You have been a good friend."

I stayed with the English for a long time. They gave me English clothes to wear. They taught me to read. They taught me about their God.

Father returned some of the prisoners. But he did not return them all. So I stayed with the English. I later met a man named John Rolfe. He visited me often.

"I love you, Pocahontas," John Rolfe told me one day. "I want to marry you."

An Englishman wanted to marry me! I was surprised at first, but I had grown fond of John Rolfe, and I realized I loved him, too. Father agreed to the marriage. So did the English governor. The governor was the chief of the English in our land, which they called Virginia.

The governor wished us happiness, but he was not stupid. He wanted peace between the English and the Powhatan. He knew that if I married John Rolfe, my father wouldn't attack the English.

The governor said I must be baptized a Christian before we could marry. I thought about this. It was a big step. But I believed what the English had taught me about their God. So I became a Christian. I took the name Rebecca, and when I was married I became Rebecca Rolfe.

Father didn't come to the wedding. It would have been too hard for him to see his daughter accepting English ways. He sent gifts, though. He also sent two of my brothers. I promised to be John Rolfe's wife, with my brothers and other members of my tribe looking on.

John Rolfe and I were happy. Soon we had a son. We named him Thomas.

When Thomas was a year old, we sailed to England. The governor wanted the people in England to meet us. Many members of my tribe went with us.

We sailed for two months. Finally we arrived in the English city called London. London was so big! It was filled with people and houses.

The governor took us to a palace in London. He took us to meet the English king and queen.

The palace was enormous. All of Father's villages could have fit into it. It was filled with paintings and tapestries and elaborately carved statues. The throne room, where the king sat, was crowded with people. Musicians played trumpets and drums and other strange instruments. I waited until the king's man called my name. "Rebecca Rolfe," he said.

I stepped forward and knelt before the king and queen. They were very kind. They asked questions about the Powhatan and seemed pleased with my answers. I think they must have adopted me into their tribe, because they invited me to a ball.

"A ball is a big party, with music and dancing," said the queen.

The king and queen invited me to many things—plays, musical concerts, dinners, and more balls. I met many people, and an artist even drew my portrait.

We stayed in England for almost a year. I loved London, but it was hard on us. We were not used to English diseases and the damp English weather.

Some of the Powhatan who had sailed to England with us became ill. Soon I began to feel sick, too.

"We need to sail home," said John Rolfe. "You cannot get better here. You will only get better at home."

So John Rolfe, Thomas, and I boarded the ship. But I was too sick to sail to America. John Rolfe carried me ashore. He called for a doctor to take care of me.

Sadly, I never made it back to America.

Robin Hood

Based on the original story by Louis Rhead

Adapted by Rebecca Grazulis

Illustrated by Marty Noble and Muriel Wood

A long time ago there lived a boy named Robin Hood. Robin's hero was his father, who was a brave knight.

"Robin," his father would say, "you must treat all people equally, no matter if they are rich or poor."

Robin took this lesson to heart, which pleased his father. His father was also pleased with Robin's archery. "You hold that bow as if you were born with it!" said Robin's father.

Marian, a young girl who lived nearby, also loved to watch Robin hit his targets. "It's amazing!" she would call out as Robin made a bull's-eye.

Robin grew older. He wanted to live on his own. "The forest is my home," he said. Robin built a hut in Sherwood Forest. He made friends with the villagers. Then he decided to join the King's Foresters.

The Foresters were led by the Sheriff of Nottingham. "I dare you to kill one of the king's deer," said the sheriff.

"It is wrong," said Robin.

The sheriff said it was safe. He lied. Robin hit a deer, and the sheriff went to arrest him. But Robin was saved by his friends.

Now, the Sheriff of Nottingham did not like looking foolish. "Who does this Robin Hood think he is?" he boomed. "Nobody makes a fool of the Sheriff of Nottingham!" The sheriff was so angry that he declared Robin Hood to be an outlaw and offered a reward for his capture.

Meanwhile, Robin Hood was growing into a strong young man, and an even better archer. He made many good friends. There was Friar Tuck, a spiritual advisor to Robin, Little John, a kind giant of a man, and Will Scarlet, an adventurous scamp. "We shall call ourselves the Merry Men!" announced Robin.

Together the Merry Men created a camp in Sherwood Forest. They built a number of tree houses joined by rope bridges, and they hollowed out the trunk of a great tree to store their bows and arrows. One day, they decided they needed a leader.

"We shall have an archery contest," said Little John. It was no surprise when Robin hit bull's-eye after bull's-eye. "Robin Hood, you are the leader of the Merry Men," declared Friar Tuck.

Robin wanted to help people. He started by telling the tax men that they should not take money from the poor. The Merry Men grabbed the tax men. Little John lifted one in the air. "Do not hurt us!" the tax men cried.

The tax men dropped their money. They said they would never take from the poor again.

Robin Hood and the Merry Men gave the money back to the poor.

"Use this to help your husband get well," said Robin Hood as he handed coins to a woman.

"Thank you, Robin Hood!" yelled all the people.

The news of the Merry Men's encounter with the tax collectors spread across the countryside. It wasn't long before even the Sheriff of Nottingham heard the story—and he was furious.

"There must be a way to catch Robin Hood," he said.

The sheriff soon came up with what he thought was a foolproof way to draw Robin Hood into the open. He would hold an archery contest.

"The winner will receive a golden arrow," declared the sheriff. He knew Robin Hood would not be able to resist. The sheriff was right. Robin Hood couldn't resist, but he knew the contest was a trap.

"Merry Men," said Robin, "the Sheriff of Nottingham is up to his old tricks. But that isn't going to keep me away from a good archery contest!"

The Merry Men looked worried. Robin Hood just laughed. "Such long faces!" he said with a wink. "Not to worry. We will wear disguises—no one will know us."

Robin Hood put a patch over one eye and dressed as a beggar. Will Scarlet became a musician and Little John a blacksmith. Even Friar Tuck got into the act and disguised himself as a baker.

Men came to the contest from all over England. "I wonder where Robin Hood is," said the sheriff.

The contest came down to two men: Hugh o' the Moors and Robin Hood. Hugh o' the Moors hit the target in the center. Robin's arrow hit Hugh's arrow and split it in half. Robin won!

The sheriff invited the winner to have dinner with him. When Robin left the sheriff's house, he turned and shot an arrow with a note on it through the window. The note read: "You dined with Robin Hood!"

One day Robin and his Merry Men came upon a young man named Allan-a-Dale in Sherwood Forest. Robin saw that he looked very sad. "My good man," said Robin, "why so melancholy?"

Allan-a-Dale sighed heavily. "The woman I love is going to marry another man," he explained. "Her father wants her to marry for money, and money I don't have. I'm only a singer and poet."

Soon the Merry Men took off toward the chapel where Allan-a-Dale's beloved was about to be married. Robin Hood jumped between the bride and the groom.

"Allan-a-Dale is the only man this bride will marry today," declared Robin Hood. Then he handed some gold coins to the bride's father. It was then that the groom realized the father had been after his money.

At this point, Friar Tuck stepped forward. "Perhaps I can be of service," he said. And that very day Friar Tuck married Allan-a-Dale to his lovely bride.

One summer day the Sheriff of Nottingham's wife asked Robin Hood to dinner. Robin Hood dressed so the sheriff would not know it was him. He loved to tease the sheriff. "Today I shot Robin Hood," said Robin. He said he would take the sheriff to see Robin Hood.

They rode into the forest. The Merry Men circled the sheriff. He knew he had been tricked!

"I am Robin Hood," said Robin. "You have been with me all along." The Merry Men took the sheriff's money and sent him on his way back home.

The Sheriff of Nottingham fumed for weeks after his encounter with Robin Hood. He decided to hold a feast for all of the best knights in England. He felt sure they would be able to help him.

"Brave knights," said the sheriff, "whoever is able to capture Robin Hood will receive a great reward."

"Sheriff," replied one of the knights, "that is impossible. Robin Hood cannot be captured." Then another knight told the sheriff of a much-feared knight named Sir Guy of Gisbourne.

"He is the man for this job," said the knight. The sheriff immediately sent word to Sir Guy, who eagerly accepted the challenge. Sir Guy soon found Robin Hood deep within Sherwood Forest.

"I am Sir Guy of Gisbourne," said Sir Guy. "I come on behalf of the Sheriff of Nottingham. Prepare to fight!"

Their swordfight lasted quite some time, but Robin prevailed. He sent Sir Guy back to the sheriff with his head bowed in shame.

Marian had not seen Robin in a long time. She went to find him. She dressed as a man because women could not walk alone in the forest. Robin did not know it was Marian. "Who are you?" he asked.

Marian did not know it was Robin. She was afraid of being robbed. Marian drew her sword. "Go away," she said. "I am looking for Robin Hood."

Robin recognized her voice. "Marian, it is I, Robin Hood!" he cried.

Soon they married. Everyone in the forest came to the wedding. "Together we will help others," Robin said to Marian. And that is exactly what they did, for the rest of their lives.

Black Beauty

Based on the original story by Anna Sewell

Adapted by Virginia R. Biles   Illustrated by Jon Goodell

I was not always called Black Beauty. I was first called Darkie because my coat was a dull black. I also had a white star on my forehead and one white foot.

My first home was very pleasant, and my mother and I spent many happy hours running side by side in the meadow. One day she said, "I want you to pay close attention to me and never forget what I am going to tell you."

I nodded my head and whinnied. "You," she continued, "must never kick or bite, not even in play. You must grow up to be gentle and good and do your work well. Most importantly, always do what your master asks you to do."

I was happy in the meadow with my mother.

When I was four, my master offered to sell me to Squire Gordon. "Train him well, and I will buy him," said Squire Gordon.

My master put a bit in my mouth. He put a saddle on my back. Then he climbed into the saddle and rode me around the meadow.

He rode me a little every day. The blacksmith nailed iron shoes to my feet. One day, I went to live at Squire Gordon's farm.

"Goodbye, Darkie," my master said. "Be a good horse and always do your best."

My coat was now shiny black, and my new master named me Black Beauty. I missed my old master and my mother, but I had two new friends, Ginger and Merrylegs. Ginger was a chestnut mare who had a bad habit of biting and snapping. That was why they called her Ginger.

The coachman, John, and the stable boy, Joe Greene, were kind to us, and I noticed that as the weeks went by, Ginger became more gentle.

Merrylegs was a kind little pony who pulled Squire Gordon's daughters in the cart and who rode the little boys on his back. One day Merrylegs was very tired, and the boys hit him with sticks to make him trot faster. "I just rose up on my hind legs," Merrylegs told me, "and let the boys slip to the ground."

"I would have bitten them," said Ginger.

"Oh, no!" said Merrylegs. "I just wanted to teach them a lesson."

I was happy at Squire Gordon's with John and Joe and my friends. One night John woke me up. "Beauty," he said, "the mistress is sick. We must ride for the doctor!"

I galloped as fast as I could. I ran through a small town. I ran through the dark woods. Finally I stopped at a house. "My mistress needs you," I heard John say.

"May I ride your horse?" said the doctor. He climbed on my back. I galloped through the dark woods. I ran through a small town. I ran down the hills. I ran up the hills. Finally I was home. I had saved my mistress's life.

When my mistress was better, Squire Gordon took her and the children to a warm country. He sold me to his friend, the Earl. The Earl renamed me Black Auster. One day while the family was away, my coachman rode me home from the village. The blacksmith told him that I had a loose shoe, but the coachman said, "It will be all right until we get home."

Ordinarily the coachman was a gentle man, but on this day I could tell something was wrong. He was in a bad temper. He began to gallop me. My shoe grew looser, and then it came off. My hoof split, and the sharp stones hurt my foot. I stumbled and fell, and the coachman crashed to the ground. Finally, help came. I heard someone say, "He is dead." I limped home, and the veterinarian bandaged my foot.

The Earl came to see me. "He is ruined as a carriage horse," he said. "I will sell him." Within a few days, I was taken to a horse fair and sold.

My new owner was Jerry. People paid Jerry to drive them places. Jerry was kind. He named me Jack. I stayed with Jerry a long time.

One New Year's Eve, two men paid Jerry to take them to a party and wait for them. Snow began to fall. My legs were cold. Jerry coughed and coughed. By the time the men came, Jerry was very sick.

The doctor told Jerry, "You must find another job." I was sold again.

This time I was sold to a man who hauled wagonloads of corn. He named me Blackie. Because he cared more for money than he did for me, I was overloaded and overworked. When I did not move fast enough for him, he whipped me. When I could not pull enough he sold me to a cab owner.

Often I would have to pull the cab loaded with men into the country, up and down steep hills, and back again. I was too tired to eat my food. My driver would whip me until he drew blood.

One day I was to take a man, woman, and two children to the train station. They had a great deal of luggage.

"Papa," I heard the little girl say, "this poor horse cannot take us and all of our luggage. Please get another cab to help."

Her father refused. I tried to do as my mother had told me, but the load was too much. I fell in the street.

I was of no use to my owner now, so he sent me to the next horse fair.

A little boy at the fair looked at me. "Look, Grandpa!" he said. "Can you buy him and make him young again?"

"I can't make old horses young," the grandfather said.

"I think he was once very beautiful," said the boy. "Please, Grandpa."

The auctioneer led me to the platform. "How much am I bid?" he called.

"I bid five pounds," said the old man.

"Sold!" said the auctioneer. The little boy named Willie happily led me home.

The grandfather gave me to Willie to care for, and I have never had better care. I had oats and hay every morning, and I ran in the meadow every day. He always had kind words for me and called me Old Crony. Sometimes he would bring me carrots and other treats. One day the grandfather said to Willie, "We will see how his legs are in the spring."

When spring came, I had improved thanks to the good food, the rest, and above all, the tender care. "We will try him on the carriage now," the grandfather said.

They hitched me up to the carriage and drove me on the country roads. I felt young and beautiful again.

"Grandfather, I am so glad you bought him," Willie said.

"So am I," the grandfather said, "but now it is time to look for a quiet place for him to live out the rest of his days with people who will treat him well."

So I was taken to my new home to pull the carriage of two older ladies.

I was led to a clean stable and fed well. My groom began to brush me. Then he looked at me again, carefully.

"White star on the forehead," he said. "White foot. Can it be Black Beauty? Do you know me? I am your old friend Joe Greene!" I looked at the man. It was my friend from long ago!

I am happy now. I take the ladies out in their carriage. I see Willie often, and my old friend Joe takes care of his Black Beauty.

Treasure Island

Based on the original story by Robert Louis Stevenson

Adapted by Leslie Lindecker   Illustrated by Julius and Victoria Lisi

My name is Jim Hawkins. This is my tale of adventure in the place known by pirates as Treasure Island.

When I was young, I helped my mother run the Admiral Benbow Inn. Our inn was on a coastal road in England.

One day an old sailor appeared at our door, dragging his sea chest behind him. His clothes were all tattered and patched. He smelled of the sea. The sailor asked for a room and paid my mother with gold coins.

The old sailor sat by the fire and watched the front door of the inn. As I walked past him, he grabbed my arm and asked, "Have ye seen a man with one leg?"

"No sir," I said. "I have not."

The old sailor stayed and stayed. One cold winter day my mother thought he was asleep.

I touched his arm. He did not move. He had passed away in his sleep.

"A fine thing!" my mother said. "He owes us money. Now all we will get is his old sea chest."

We opened the wooden chest. Inside was an old map of an island. Someone had marked one spot with an **X**.

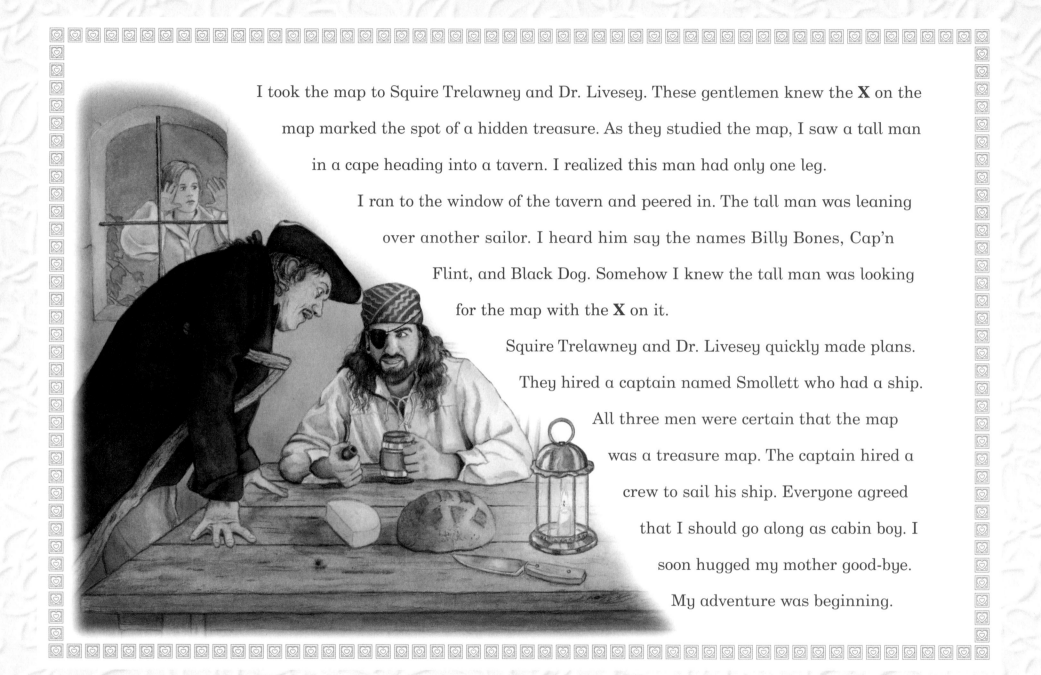

I took the map to Squire Trelawney and Dr. Livesey. These gentlemen knew the **X** on the map marked the spot of a hidden treasure. As they studied the map, I saw a tall man in a cape heading into a tavern. I realized this man had only one leg.

I ran to the window of the tavern and peered in. The tall man was leaning over another sailor. I heard him say the names Billy Bones, Cap'n Flint, and Black Dog. Somehow I knew the tall man was looking for the map with the **X** on it.

Squire Trelawney and Dr. Livesey quickly made plans. They hired a captain named Smollett who had a ship. All three men were certain that the map was a treasure map. The captain hired a crew to sail his ship. Everyone agreed that I should go along as cabin boy. I soon hugged my mother good-bye. My adventure was beginning.

We sailed late in the day. I met the ship's cook. His name was Long John Silver.

I knew Long John Silver was the man with one leg I saw at the tavern! But he was kind to me.

One night I hid in a barrel so I could hear Long John talk to some sailors. I quickly found out they were pirates!

Long John said the hidden treasure was a chest full of gold. The pirates were going to take the gold and get rid of the captain, the squire, and the doctor.

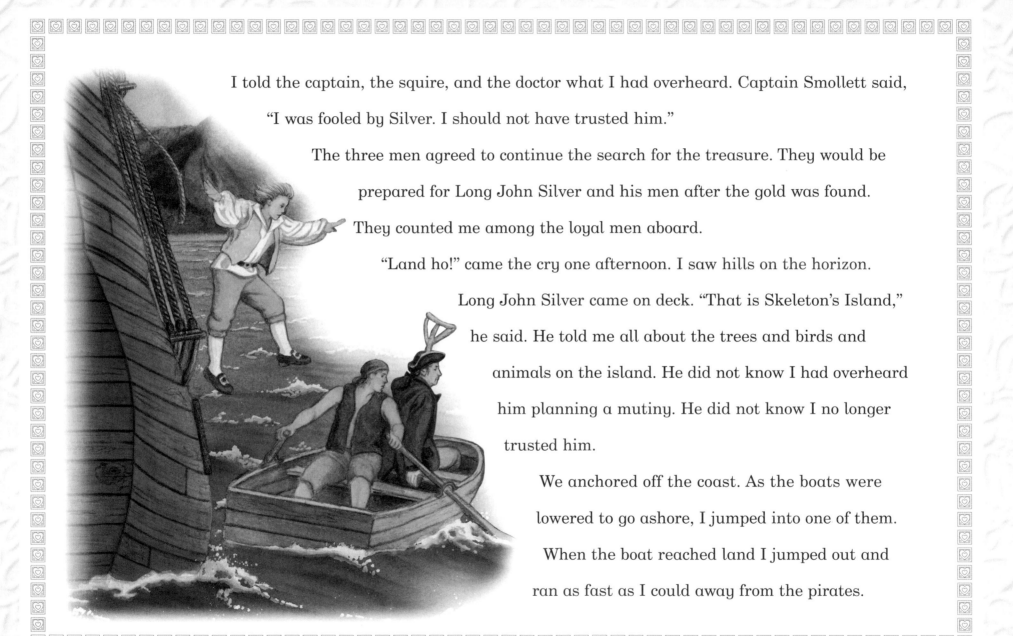

I told the captain, the squire, and the doctor what I had overheard. Captain Smollett said, "I was fooled by Silver. I should not have trusted him."

The three men agreed to continue the search for the treasure. They would be prepared for Long John Silver and his men after the gold was found. They counted me among the loyal men aboard.

"Land ho!" came the cry one afternoon. I saw hills on the horizon.

Long John Silver came on deck. "That is Skeleton's Island," he said. He told me all about the trees and birds and animals on the island. He did not know I had overheard him planning a mutiny. He did not know I no longer trusted him.

We anchored off the coast. As the boats were lowered to go ashore, I jumped into one of them. When the boat reached land I jumped out and ran as fast as I could away from the pirates.

I started to explore the island, and I came across a man named Ben Gunn. Pirates had left him on the island three years before!

The captain, the squire, and the doctor also came ashore. They soon found a small fort.

Ben Gunn and I looked for the captain, the squire, and the doctor.

We found them bringing supplies from the ship to the fort.

All of us, except Ben, waited at the fort for Long John Silver and his men.

The next morning Long John Silver was outside the fort under a flag of truce. He offered a trade. "I want the treasure map," Silver said. "I guarantee safe passage back to England for Smollett, Trelawney, Livesey, and everyone loyal to you in exchange for the map."

The captain refused to bargain with Long John Silver. Silver and all of his men would have to surrender to him. Silver became angry. He threatened to fire on the fort with the captain's own cannons on the ship. Silver then left the fort and headed for the ship.

I was restless inside the fort. I filled my pockets with biscuits and cheese for Ben Gunn and snuck out. I had a plan. I found Ben, and he led me to a small boat he had built. Under the cover of darkness I rowed out to the big ship. Quietly I began to cut away the rope holding the anchor.

I cut through the rope. Then I climbed up the part of the rope that was still tied to the ship.

I climbed over the rail and onto the deck. I quickly tied up each of the pirates as they slept.

The ship drifted into a small bay and settled next to the shoreline. The pirates on shore would not know where the big ship had gone.

I climbed back over the rail and dropped into the shallow water. I waded to shore.

Soon I approached the fort. Suddenly strong arms grabbed me from behind. I heard a strange voice calling out, "Pieces of eight! Pieces of eight!" It was Long John Silver's parrot. His men had stormed the fort and now controlled it. I was captured.

I spoke up bravely. "Your plans are ruined," I said. "Your ship is gone. You have no food."

"But I have the map," said Silver. "The captain and the others traded it for their lives."

"What good will that do?" I asked.

"There will always be another ship," said Long John Silver. The next morning we began to follow the map to the spot with the **X**. Long John Silver kept a rope tied about my waist. He was afraid I would run away.

Eventually Silver and his pirates found the place that was marked with the **X** on the map.

There was a big hole where the gold should have been. The pirates jumped into the hole. They began to fight.

Suddenly the captain and his loyal men surrounded them!

"It's over, Long John Silver!" Captain Smollett said. "Ben Gunn found the gold two years ago. He is a rich man. You are going to jail."

But Silver got away before we sailed home. To this day, when I hear "Pieces of eight," I still think of Long John Silver.

King Arthur

Based on the original story by Sir Thomas Malory

Adapted by Rebecca Grazulis   Illustrated by Edward V. Kadunc

A long time ago, a good and generous king named Uther Pendragon ruled over Britain. One of

Uther's good friends was Merlin the Wise. Merlin advised the king on many matters,

and Uther listened carefully. After all, Merlin could predict the future.

One day, Uther's greatest dream came true—his son was born. "He will be a

good man," declared Uther. "I will teach him well."

Unfortunately, on this very same day, Merlin foresaw Uther's death.

"I must find someone to take care of my son," said Uther.

"Do not worry," replied Merlin. "He will be safe in my hands." Merlin

brought the child to another family who raised him as their own. Soon Uther

Pendragon was wounded in battle and died.

The British people fought over who should be king. Many men wanted to be the new king. The fighting lasted eighteen years.

Merlin wanted the fighting to stop, so he planned a contest. It would bring together all the men of Britain. One of those men would be Uther's son.

Merlin went into a clearing in a thick forest. He stuck a sword deep into a great stone.

"Whoever can pull out this sword," said Merlin, "is the son of Uther. He will be king."

As soon as Merlin announced the contest, all the lords and all of their sons became very excited. The fighting stopped immediately, and everyone started their journey to the forest.

Merlin greeted them as they arrived. "Welcome!" shouted Merlin. "Thank you for coming. While we are waiting for all to arrive, let us have a tournament-at-arms."

Sir Ector reached the forest just in time to hear Merlin's announcement. Sir Ector had two sons—Sir Kay and Arthur. Sir Kay was the elder. He was tall and dark and had already proven himself to be a great knight. Arthur adored his brother and helped him whenever he could.

"Kay," said Sir Ector, "why don't you enter the tournament? Arthur will assist you as esquire-at-arms."

Sir Kay strode gallantly onto the battlefield. Arthur walked close behind, carrying his brother's spear and pennant.

Charge! Both sides of the battlefield ran swiftly toward one another. Sir Kay was especially courageous. When he stepped off the battlefield, Sir Ector said, "My son, I am so proud of you." But nobody was more proud of Sir Kay than his brother Arthur.

"You did well," Arthur told his brother.

"Thank you," said Sir Kay. "But my sword broke in two on the battlefield."

"Do not worry," replied Arthur. "I will find you another one." Arthur ran to get his father's sword. He found it, but he could not find his father. He did not want to take the sword without asking.

Arthur ran faster. He came to a clearing. There was the sword in the stone! Arthur could only think of helping his brother. He walked to the stone and pulled out the sword.

Arthur presented the sword to his brother. "Thank you, Arthur," said Sir Kay. "You do our family proud." Arthur was pleased with the compliment, and his happiness grew when he saw Sir Kay perform even better in the tournament's second assault. He felt like he had played a small part in his brother's success.

After the tournament ended, Sir Kay rode over to his father and his brother. He noticed that Merlin was standing with them. "You have been helped by a powerful sword, Sir Kay," said Merlin.

For the first time, Sir Kay looked carefully at the sword. It certainly was beautiful.

"Do you know who its owner is?" asked Merlin.

Sir Kay shook his head. Suddenly Arthur spoke up. He was afraid that Sir Kay was going to be punished for stealing the sword.

"I found the sword," said Arthur bravely. "It was in a clearing stuck deep in a stone. I did not mean to cause any harm. I just wanted to help my brother."

Merlin put his arm around Arthur's shoulders. "I know," said Merlin. "Let's talk privately in my tent."

Merlin handed the sword to Arthur. "This sword is yours," said Merlin. "That was the contest. Everyone would try to lift the sword from the stone."

Merlin paused. "Sir Ector is not your father," Merlin said. Arthur was stunned. "Your father was Uther Pendragon. This was his sword. He knew that there would be fighting in Britain after he died. He wanted you to be safe."

"So Sir Ector made me his son to protect me," said Arthur. "And Sir Kay and I played together like brothers."

"Yes," said Merlin.

Suddenly Arthur realized that Sir Kay was standing by his side. He had obviously heard everything that Merlin had said, as his expression was one of shock. "I can't believe it," said Sir Kay.

Arthur noticed that Sir Kay was trembling a bit, so he reached out and put his hand on his brother's shoulder. "I know, brother," said Arthur. "I can hardly believe it myself."

Soon Merlin started to explain what would happen next. "We must still have the contest," said Merlin.

"But why?" asked Arthur.

"You are the rightful king of Britain," said Merlin, "but you must prove it to all the lords so they will accept you. Tomorrow they will know that you are the only true heir."

"Tomorrow … tomorrow I will be king … ," said Arthur, amazed.

At these words, Sir Kay cried out in pain. Arthur turned to him, genuinely concerned for the brother he greatly admired.

"Do not worry," said Arthur. "We will always be brothers."

But Sir Kay could not speak. He felt deeply jealous of Arthur. Sir Kay thought Arthur would always assist him. He met Arthur's eyes and then turned and left the tent.

"He wanted to be king," said Merlin. "He is jealous."

"No!" said Arthur. "My brother is a good man."

"Even good men can be bad sometimes," said Merlin. Arthur looked sad. He did not want to lose his family.

"Arthur, you must get ready for the contest tomorrow," said Merlin.

Arthur went home to sleep. But Arthur had trouble sleeping. He kept thinking of his brother. He wanted Sir Kay by his side. But Sir Kay did not come home that night and could not be found the next morning.

The next day Sir Ector walked with Arthur to the gathering place. Even though his victory was sure, Arthur was nervous. He knew in his heart that he was the son of Uther Pendragon, but he was still very young to be king. Was he really ready for such a job?

"I have loved being your father," said Sir Ector. "I always felt that Merlin gave me a great gift when he brought you to my doorstep. But it is hard to say good-bye."

"This isn't good-bye, Father," replied Arthur. "We will see each other, and I hope we will see Kay."

"Yes," said Sir Ector, "but let us walk slowly to the gathering place anyway."

When they reached the gathering place it was filled with the lords of Britain. Arthur swallowed hard when he saw the crowd. There were even more people there than he had imagined there would be.

Merlin soon spotted Arthur in the crowd. Then he announced the contest's rules.

"Great lords of Britain!" called Merlin. "Your task is now set. Whoever can pull the sword from the anvil upon this mighty stone is the true king of Britain!"

One by one, each man tried to pull out the sword. No one could do it. "It is too hard, Merlin!" they cried.

"It is not too hard for the true king!" said Merlin. The men started to grumble.

Then Arthur stepped up to the stone. He grabbed the sword and pulled it out quickly. He held it above his head for everyone to see.

The crowd was quiet. Suddenly a voice called out, "You are my king, Arthur!"

It was Sir Kay. He slowly dropped to one knee. Soon every man was kneeling before Arthur, the true king of Britain.

Heidi

Based on the original story by Johanna Spyri

Adapted by Lisa Harkrader   Illustrated by Linda Dockey Graves

"Grandfather?" said Heidi as she tried to smile. "It's me. Heidi." Heidi watched the old man. She wondered if the villagers were right about him. What if he really was mean?

Heidi had lived all her life with her Aunt Detie. But now Detie had taken a job with a family in the city, and Heidi couldn't go along. She was sent to the mountains to live with her grandfather. The old man stared at her. "You have your mother's eyes," he said.

"Is that bad?" said Heidi.

"No," said her grandfather. "It's good. Very good."

He opened his arms wide, and Heidi fell into them. It was the first hug she'd had in a very long time.

Heidi loved the mountains. She loved Grandfather's cabin. One day, a herd of goats ran past the cabin. A boy ran after them. "Come back!" yelled the boy.

The goats kept on running. "Who is that?" Heidi asked her grandfather.

"That is Peter," said Grandfather. "He takes care of the goats from the village." Peter shouted again. The goats kept running.

"Peter tries hard," said Grandfather. "But the goats do not listen to him."

"I could help," said Heidi. "I would like to take care of the goats."

Heidi helped Peter round up the goats. They took them to a pasture high on the mountain and watched them graze. "Where do you live?" Heidi asked Peter.

"I live halfway down the mountain with my mother and grandmother," said Peter. "Mother works in the village. Granny used to do mending for the villagers, but now she's blind and too sick."

"She must be lonely," said Heidi. "Maybe I could visit her."

"She'd like that," said Peter. The next morning, Heidi skipped down the mountain to Peter's house and met his mother and grandmother.

"She came especially to see you," Peter told Granny.

Granny clapped her hands. "It's been so long since anyone visited," said Granny. Heidi pulled a stool close to Granny's chair. The wind howled through the little house. A shutter banged against the outside wall. "This house is so old," Granny sighed.

Soon Heidi heard another kind of banging. She peeked out the window. "It's Grandfather!" she said.

Grandfather was standing on a ladder, hammering a nail into the loose shutter to keep it from banging in the wind.

Heidi visited Granny every day. Grandfather visited, too. He fixed the roof. He fixed the windows. He fixed the squeaky door.

One morning, Heidi and Grandfather heard a knock at their door. Heidi opened it. Aunt Detie came in.

"Pack your things," Aunt Detie told Heidi. "We have to catch the train."

Aunt Detie told Heidi her plan. "You are going to the city. You will live with a wealthy family. You will help their daughter."

Grandfather was upset. "Heidi is not leaving," he said.

Aunt Detie tried to convince Grandfather that going to the city would be best for Heidi. "The family in the city has a tutor," said Aunt Detie. "Heidi will get a good education. You won't deny her that, will you?"

Grandfather shook his head. "Get your things, Heidi. You have a train to catch."

Heidi and Aunt Detie rode the train to the city. When they arrived, a carriage took them to a huge house. A servant showed them into the library. Heidi heard a squeaking sound, and a wheelchair rolled into the room. Sitting in the chair was a pale, frail-looking girl with lovely long curls.

"You must be Heidi," said the girl. "I'm Clara."

Heidi and Clara soon became close friends. Heidi told Clara about her life on the mountain. "In the summer Peter and I go to the high pasture and lie in the grass. In the winter we sled down the mountain."

"Sounds wonderful," said Clara.

Clara's grandmother read stories to Clara and Heidi. Heidi learned the alphabet. She learned words. Soon she learned how to read.

Clara's doctor came once a week. "Your cheeks get more pink every day," Dr. Classen told Clara. "Heidi is good for you." The doctor looked at Heidi. "But Heidi, you are thin and pale. Do you feel sick?"

"I am fine," said Heidi.

"She is not fine," said Clara. "She barely eats. And she does not sleep."

"I eat enough," said Heidi, "and I sleep enough."

"I'm fine," said Heidi. "Truly." Heidi didn't want Clara and her grandmother to think she didn't like living with them. But that night Heidi awoke with a start. She found herself lying in the hall, surrounded by Clara, Clara's grandmother, and Dr. Classen.

"Heidi!" cried Clara. "Thank goodness you're all right!"

Dr. Classen patted Heidi's hand. "Heidi was sleepwalking," he said. "I'm afraid city life doesn't agree with her. The only cure is to send Heidi home to the mountains."

Clara nodded. "Dr. Classen is right," she said. "I'll miss you, but I can't keep you from the mountains you love. I'll write to you, though."

The next day, Heidi rode the train back to the mountains. When Heidi arrived at Grandfather's cabin, he was waiting outside.

"Heidi!" said Grandfather as he pulled her into his arms and hugged her tight. "My Heidi is home."

That night Heidi slept in her hay bed. She didn't toss and turn, and she didn't walk in her sleep.

Grandfather woke Heidi early the next morning. "You cannot miss school," he said. "I found a house in the village. We will live there in the winter. Then you can go to school."

Heidi and Grandfather carried everything they needed down the mountain to their new house. Heidi and Grandfather lived in the village all winter. Peter came down every morning. He and Heidi walked to school together.

When summer finally came, Heidi and Grandfather went back up the mountain. They stayed in their cabin all summer.

One day, a letter arrived for Heidi from the city. She tore it open and read it aloud:

Dear Heidi,

Dr. Classen says I'm strong enough for a visit in the mountains. Grandmama and I will arrive by train at the end of the month. I can't wait to see you.

Love,

Clara

"A month!" said Heidi. "I'll see Clara and her grandmother in a month!"

Heidi spent the next month getting ready for Clara's visit. She took down the curtains and washed them, and she stuffed fresh straw in the mattress on her bed. One day as Heidi was outside shaking the rugs, she spotted a group of people coming up the mountain—a woman rolling a wheelchair, and two men carrying a girl with long curls.

"They're here!" Heidi shouted. "Two men from the village have brought Clara and Grandmama!" Heidi dropped the rugs in the grass and scrambled down the path.

"Clara, I'm so happy to see you!" said Heidi.

"I'm happy to see you, too!" said Clara. "And I love your mountains."

Clara stayed in the cabin with Heidi. She drank fresh goat milk. She ate fresh goat cheese. She spent her days with Heidi and Peter.

"Clara, you look so much better," Grandmama said one morning. Clara, Heidi, and Peter smiled. "We have a surprise for you, Grandmama," said Clara.

Heidi held one of Clara's arms. Peter held the other. Clara stood up. She took a step toward Grandmama. Then another step. Then another.

"Clara!" said Grandmama. "You are walking!"

Grandmama hugged Clara. "Heidi is good for you," she said. "And Heidi's mountains are good for you, too."

The Three Musketeers

Based on the original story by Alexandre Dumas

Adapted by Suzanne Lieurance   Illustrated by John Lund

D'Artagnan was a young man who lived in France. It was time for him to leave home and make his way in the world. "All I have to give you are fifteen gold coins, this letter to Captain Treville, and my old horse," said his father.

"Treville is the captain of the musketeers and my good friend," continued d'Artagnan's father. "Take him this letter. See if you, too, can become a musketeer."

D'Artagnan's greatest wish was to join the musketeers, the soldiers who guarded King Louis of France. Now, perhaps his wish would come true. D'Artagnan strapped on his sword, mounted the old horse, and started out for Paris.

D'Artagnan stopped at an inn to eat. A dark-haired man with a scar laughed. "Don't laugh at my horse," said d'Artagnan.

"Go away," said the man. D'Artagnan raced toward him. The innkeeper hit d'Artagnan over the head and knocked him out.

The man with the scar grabbed the letter to Treville. "I bet Treville sent this young man to ruin my plan," he said.

D'Artagnan woke up. The man with the scar was talking to a woman he called Milady. "I'm leaving for Paris," he told her.

"I'll find you in Paris!" d'Artagnan yelled at the man.

When d'Artagnan got to Paris he went to Treville's office. Treville was talking to two musketeers, Porthos and Aramis. "The cardinal reported that three of my men nearly started a riot yesterday," said Treville. "His guards had to arrest them. Where is Athos?"

"It wasn't our fault, sir," said Porthos. "The cardinal's guards attacked us. Athos was wounded, but we fought well and escaped."

Treville smiled. "I am proud of you for fighting so bravely, but you must not risk your lives foolishly."

Athos soon arrived and was treated by a doctor. Treville asked d'Artagnan, "Why have you come to see me?"

"To join the musketeers," said d'Artagnan. "I had a letter from my father, who is a friend of yours. But a coward with a scar stole the letter."

"A scar? Why, that man is Count Rochefort!" said Treville. "And he is up to no good."

D'Artagnan thought he saw Count Rochefort outside. He raced after him and ran right into Porthos, Aramis, and Athos. "We should teach you some manners," said Porthos. D'Artagnan drew his sword. Then four of the cardinal's guards arrived.

"You are under arrest for dueling," said a guard.

"There are four guards, but only three of us," said Athos.

D'Artagnan smiled. "There are four of us, not three." The four friends defeated the guards. Then they marched arm in arm down the street.

Treville heard about the musketeers' battle with the guards. "I'm sure the guards picked the fight with you," he said. "I know you would not fight needlessly."

Even the king was pleased at what the four young men had done. The cardinal was his adviser, but the king did not want the cardinal to feel too powerful. The king summoned the four young men to the palace.

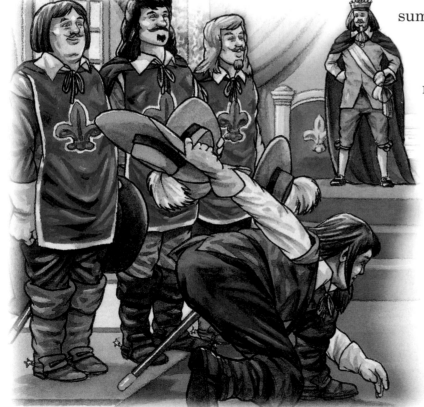

"So, you are the brave fellow who fought so well with my musketeers," the king said as he handed forty gold pieces to d'Artagnan. "This is your reward."

D'Artagnan bowed and thanked the king. Then he left the palace. D'Artagnan felt rich. He found a place to live and hired a servant to work for him. During the day d'Artagnan trained to be a soldier. He hoped that before long he would become a real musketeer.

Soon all the gold pieces were gone. D'Artagnan was now penniless.

One day d'Artagnan's landlord came to visit. "My wife, Constance, has been kidnapped," said the landlord. "She works for the queen. The Duke of Buckingham loves the queen. The cardinal feels this might be dangerous for the king, so he spies on the queen.

"Count Rochefort and his men took my wife to learn the queen's secrets. Please rescue my wife. You can live here for free if you do."

That night, d'Artagnan heard noises coming from his landlord's apartment. It was Constance. She had escaped, but Count Rochefort and his men had found her. D'Artagnan chased the men away and rescued Constance.

The cardinal spoke with Count Rochefort. Rochefort told the cardinal that the queen had given the duke a sash with twelve diamond studs on it. The king had recently given the queen these diamonds as a gift.

"Perfect," said the cardinal. "I shall write to Milady in London and tell her to steal two of the diamond studs and bring them to me. The queen will be disgraced!"

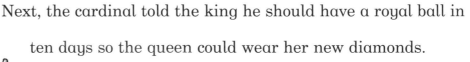

Next, the cardinal told the king he should have a royal ball in ten days so the queen could wear her new diamonds.

"What shall I do?" the queen said to Constance. "I gave the diamonds to the duke. The cardinal must know this, and he plans to disgrace me."

"My husband will get the diamonds back," Constance said. "Write a letter to the duke in London so he will know someone is coming for the diamonds."

But Constance's husband refused to deliver the queen's letter to the duke. D'Artagnan told Constance that he and the three musketeers would deliver the letter.

D'Artagnan and the musketeers took the letter and rode out of Paris. Porthos and Athos got into a fight with an innkeeper. D'Artagnan and Aramis had to leave them. Later, some men on the road fired guns at d'Artagnan and Aramis. Aramis was wounded. D'Artagnan had to leave him, too.

D'Artagnan finally made it to the ship that would take him to the duke. Count Rochefort was there. D'Artagnan fought the count. He defeated the count and got on the ship.

The next morning the ship arrived in England. D'Artagnan quickly raced to the duke's mansion with the letter from the queen.

The duke read the letter, then he took d'Artagnan to a hidden room where he kept the sash with the diamonds on it. Two of the diamonds were missing. "I don't understand," said the duke. "The only time I wore this sash was at a ball a week ago. Milady was there. She must have stolen the diamonds for the cardinal!"

The duke ordered two more diamonds from his jeweler, and D'Artagnan took them back to France. He arrived just as the ball was about to begin. He saw the cardinal hand the king a box. It had two diamonds in it. "If the queen is missing two diamonds, Sire, show her these," said the cardinal.

The queen entered, wearing all twelve diamonds. The cardinal saw d'Artagnan talking to Constance. He realized they had outsmarted him, so he lied to the king. "I wanted to give two diamonds to the queen, but I did not want to present them myself," said the cardinal. Then he told Milady that she must make d'Artagnan pay for ruining his plan.

"Kill Constance!" the cardinal told Milady. She agreed to do it, but only if the cardinal would write a letter saying she could do anything for the good of France.

The queen hid Constance. Milady and d'Artagnan each found out where she was. Milady offered Constance some poisoned wine. D'Artagnan rushed in. Constance dropped the glass as she was about to take a sip.

The cardinal was afraid to make d'Artagnan his enemy, so he made him a musketeer. Now D'Artagnan's greatest wish had finally come true!

The End